C0-CFI-046

Sweet Memories

The Lagomarcino Story

Sweet Memories

The Lagomarcino Story

By Bill Wundram

With thanks to ...

Terry Wilson, who coordinated this whole box of chocolates

Rebecca Heidgerken, graphic designer

Photography by Gregory Boll

Contributed photos by Terry Otten, Daniel Otten,
Harry Lamon, Moline Dispatch Publishing Co., Gil Cervelli and Mike Newell

Tom Heidgerken, color specialist

Joe Kelley, illustrator

Deborah Brasier, editor

Sweet Memories:
The Lagomarcino Story

Written by Bill Wundram

© Copyright 2008

Published by Lagomarcino's
2132 East 11th Street
Davenport, IA 52803
Phone: (563) 324-6137

ISBN 10: 1-59152-053-3
ISBN 13: 978-1-59152-053-5

Printed in the U.S.A.

To Angelo and Luigia,
our grandparents
who started it all

To Uncle Charlie & Aunt Mary,
Joe & Anita Schenone,
for all their hard work and dedication

To Mom & Dad,
Betsy & Tom Lagomarcino,
who have guided us to where we are today

Beth Lagomarcino
Tom Lagomarcino, Jr.
Ann Lagomarcino
Paul Lagomarcino
Lisa Lagomarcino Ambrose
Carol Lagomarcino Babcock

Table of Contents

Telling 100 years of Sweet Memories

Always, chocolate. First, there is the essence of chocolate when you step through the doors of Lagomarcino's. It is ecstatic.

For a century, Lagomarcino's has been with us … a tradition in a family that fits together like bon bons in a box of chocolates. It makes you think that there is nothing better than a good friend, unless it is a friend with a box of chocolates from Lagomarcino's.

Lagomarcino's is an emotion. It is a taste. It is a thick malted milk and a soda with two straws.

All of MidAmerica experiences ownership in Lago's and its ice cream parlors in Moline, Illinois, and Davenport, Iowa. They are not drive-throughs. They are the real thing.

Customers are like family … generations of customers embrace the two places. So do the national magazines. When Douglas Brinkley was in town to write about the Mississippi River for National Geographic Traveler, he was told, "Don't leave until you have a hot fudge sundae at Lagomarcino's." He complied — and said that sundae was the best in the world.

All the world loves Lagomarcino's. Its chocolates are shipped by the tens of thousands to faraway places with strange-sounding names. A military pilot from Davenport passes a box of Lago chocolates to his crew while on a mission over Iraq and tells them, "It reminds me of home."

All of this is an affirmation of faith. It is like the customer who said, "If I were in prison, and it was my last meal, I'd order a Lagomarcino's egg salad on their rye bread."

One day, Tom Lagomarcino Jr. called: "In 2008, it will be our hundredth anniversary, and I …"

I didn't allow him to finish the sentence. "I think you want me to write a book."

We worked over thousands of words and hundreds of photos. "Be sure to get in that secret one of you," he insisted. I objected. We laughed. I'm hidden in the crowd on one of the pages. It is one of those "Where's Waldo?" things.

After it was completed I said, "Here is your book."

Tom said, "No, it is *our* book."

I had been adopted as a part of the family.

Bill Wundram

To our customers:

This book is a sweet story of how our
customers have touched our hearts and allowed us to
be a part of their lives for the past 100 years.
Thank you for sharing nearly 1,000 memories that
made us smile, cry and laugh out loud.

Family portrait, the Moline store, early days: Angelo, little Tom in front of Luigia; Mary and Charlie, all Lagomarcinos. The place has changed little from then to the present.

In the beginning, there was a town in Italy …

In the sunny hills outside Genoa, Italy, there is a town called Lagomarsino. It climbs, step by step, in the foothills of the Apennines. Translated, it means "Lake in March," or, loosely interpreted, "when the snow melts."

Angelo Lagomarcino may have intended to spell his name "Lagomarsino," for his home village, but in the translation of immigrating into the United States, the "s" apparently became a "c" and there has never been an inclination to correct it.

In 1908, Angelo and his wife, Luigia, came to Moline, Illinois, by train

1

Angelo Lagomarcino, in the early days of the Moline store.

Luigia at the cigar case, about 1920.

to open a little store at 1422 Fifth Avenue. It was to be a confectionary, with an assortment of other items on the shelves and in the glass cases. One big window said, "Ice Cream and Candy." The other, "Cigars and Tobacco." Luigia was often behind the tobacco counter, rolling dice — double or nothing — for cigars, cigarettes and plug tobacco.

Angelo sold sweets, but cherished fruit, carefully shaping pyramids of shiny apples and oranges in the streetfront showcases and cutting bananas — using an odd-shaped crooked knife — from 4-foot bunches hanging in the windows. Italians treasure fruit, and Angelo polished every single apple to a mirror shine. Usually, he

Lagomarcino tokens, used for purchases in the early 1900s.

polished them with his apron.

There were three children, Charlie, Mary and Tom Sr. Along came a cousin, Joe Schenone, and his wife, Anita. All were quickly involved in the business.

Mary and Tom, though, were the heart of the Moline store.

Tom Sr. wed Betsy Pinch and they had six children — Beth, Tom Jr., Ann, Paul, Lisa and Carol. All worked behind the counters and soda fountain.

The Moline store flourished, but times and habits change.

"The 100-year-old Moline place was like a one-lane bowling alley," says Tom Jr. To survive, the business had to grow and expand to the Iowa Quad-Cities.

Happy Joe Whitty suggested that the Lagomarcinos turn his place in the Village of East Davenport — a building that once housed Smith's Pharmacy —into a classy soda fountain. The address was 2132 East 11th Street. Lagomarcino's has been there, happily ever after, since 1997.

Now, with two Lagomarcino Soda Fountains, the patriarch — Angelo, in the black wrist-to-elbow sleevelets — likely would be very pleased.

He would clap his hands and shout, "Ura! Ura!"

That is Italian for "Joy!"

Long ago … Mary, Tom and Charlie Lagomarcino.

Mary Lagomarcino and Tom Jr. in front of the Moline store, 1921. Note the trolley in the background.

Tom Lagomarcino Sr.

A tradition dipped in chocolate

In the store on Fifth Avenue in Moline, Tom Lagomarcino Sr., 92, stands alongside a counter of sweets. His green eyes twinkle. He was born with a smile. He has adjusted his crisp white apron and neatly ties the strings in a bow in the back.

"The apron is my robe of office," he says. It reaches below his knees. It is

Tom Sr., 1965, dapper in a vest in the Moline store.

"Yes, I remember Tommy," former employee Bill Meeds of Santa Rosa, Calif., says of Tom Sr. "He was the young, good-looking Italian that all the girls came in to see. They didn't talk to me if he was there. You see, there is only three years' difference in our age. I am 89." Tom Sr. is 92.

hard to imagine Tom without an apron.

He pushes back the bridge of his glasses and claps his hands. Life is his joy, chocolate is his god-given relative.

His dad, Angelo, always wore an apron, too. It was a tremendous leap of faith that led him, in 1908, to travel from northern Italy and open a little confectionary in a town he knew only as "John Deere factory."

Tom Sr. presses lean fingers to his lips and speaks with admiration of his dad's courage.

"It took sheer guts. He didn't know the language, couldn't speak English."

Angelo worked hard. His family worked hard. Relatives who followed from Italy worked hard. There were no days off.

Lagomarcino's prospered. It became a downtown Moline institution.

The family lived upstairs. When too many customers packed the store, Angelo would bang on a pipe or thump the ceiling with a long pole. It was the signal for someone to come downstairs and wait on customers.

That was a long time ago. What of today?

Tom Sr. laughs, tapping an index finger to his forehead. He tightens his necktie, which he ties with a short tail so it doesn't dip into any sodas or sundaes he's making. He doesn't appear to have forgotten anything that has happened in his long life.

At the back door of the Moline soda fountain, Angelo and Tom, about 1922.

"Everything is still going, somehow or other. Now, we're in Moline and Davenport. Lagomarcino's is a family thing. I expect it to keep on going. Everybody pulls or pushes the wagon."

He leans far back to look up and admire the ceiling of the Moline store. "Same tin ceiling; everything's the same in this place.

"By never changing, we will always remain different," he says. "Never changing is my motto."

America's sweet tooth has agreed. Tom Sr. pops his buttons to show copies of national magazines that repeatedly acclaim Lago's as the best soda fountain in all the U.S. of A.

"Customers like it old in here," he says. "Can you imagine, someone wanted us to doll up the place. Flowered ceiling and fluorescent lights. They wanted to paint the booths white. Why, it would look like a beauty salon."

Tom Sr. is eating a dish of ice cream. Chocolate is his favorite. A customer tells him, "I've never been in this place before."

He asks, "Where have you been for 100 years?"

Prohibition and the hidden closet under the sidewalk

Razz-ma-tazz. Prohibition. Sheiks and shebas. Slinky flappers in heels and short skirts and puffing Camels in long pearl cigarette holders …

She giggles. She and her beau had just been to Moline's Bio movie house two blocks from Lagomarcino's to see Rudolph Valentino in "The Sheik."

At Lago's soda fountain, the boyfriend orders "Two Green Rivers, please." The girlfriend winks, long lashes. His eyes cautiously roam the place before reaching into his tweed suit coat for a thin pint bottle of hooch. He leans over the marble-topped booth to spike her Green River. His hand slips. Crash! The bottle of bathtub gin falls in a shatter to the hard terrazo tile floor.

"Oh, how they would try to sneak in alky, and when they would drop the bottle, it broke and would stink up the place … just like this was a speakeasy," says Tom Sr. "We got out the mops and soap in a hurry."

Lago's tried to stop the spiking of innocent soda fountain drinks — root beer, lemon phosphate, Green River. It didn't always work. Atop a 1928 menu for sodas and sundaes was the warning:

> "To avoid embarrassment,
> do not attempt to mix
> intoxicating beverages
> on these premises."

There were speakeasies — dark, sleazy places in the Tri-Cities — but soda fountains had replaced the bars.

"We tried to keep guys from spiking our drinks, but it didn't always work," Tom Sr. remembers. "Guys carried flasks, fancy silver ones in their coat vest pockets, or maybe just a pint bottle of hooch. They'd pass the bottle or flask under the table or booth.

9

"I'll say this, Prohibition was the most interesting time of my life."

Tom Sr. laughs out loud to tell of Uncle Charlie.

"When random visitors full of hooch staggered in, Uncle Charlie would politely escort them out the door and point them in a westerly direction. The wind came from the west, and he said that might sober them up.

"It's bizarre today, but during Prohibition, everything was going on. There was so much hanky-panky. There was a hardware store across the alley with a fine tinsmith. Trucks backed up every night to pick up the stills he made. Stills were big on the Rock River. Every houseboat had a still; they floated alcohol downstream in barrels. That was the delivery system."

Lago's never sold beer or booze, but there was an ample supply of grapes in the basement to make wine.

"It was always for family consumption," Tom Sr. says, with a little wink. "Trucks unloaded the grapes right to the presses in the basement."

Thirty years ago, workers were pounding open the sidewalk in front of the Moline store to make more room for storage in the building.

"Look what we found," one of the workers called out. They uncovered a hidden closet with a cache of wine inside. The door was jammed by bricks, but family members wedged it open to peek inside. It was full of bottles of wine.

The wine is still there, dusty and untouched.

Cold Sandwiches

Boiled Ham   10

Pimento Cheese   10

Swiss Cheese   10

Longhorn Cheese   10

Peanut Butter   10

Hot Drinks

Coffee   05

Hot Malted Milk   15

Hot Chocolate   10

Milk   05

Specials

Fresh Peach Sundae   20

Hot Butterscotch pecan   25

"   "   "   salted almond   25

"   "   "   walnut   25

Hot fudge pecan   25

"   "   salted almond   25

"   "   walnut   25

One half Grapefruit   15

Love in the back booth

Their eyes met across a crowded soda fountain that was filled with happy customers digging into fancy sundaes called Hawaiian Twilights and Sweethearts.

Friends had told Betsy Pinch that she should meet Tom Lagomarcino Sr. Debonair, smooth, they said he was the most eligible bachelor in town.

"They told me I would go ga-ga over this Italian," Betsy says, "so I sat down in a booth and he waited on me. Oh my, he was handsome."

He served her a strawberry soda, which she remembers had an especially big dollop of whipped cream on top.

Tom Sr. and Betsy on their wedding day.

Betsy was a medical librarian at Moline Public Hospital. She remembers, "He was a handsome fellow, but at first I didn't want to get serious because I couldn't pronounce his last name, much less spell it."

He courted her in his suave Italian way. There were dinners at the Plantation, the grandest night club in what then was the Tri-Cities.

"I was impressed. He was 31," Betsy says. She is younger, and to ask her age is like drawing a line in the sand that is not to be crossed.

"I thought she was a pretty gal, and a nice gal," Tom says.

When Tom proposed, he warned: "Honey, this is going to be a challenging life for you."

He told her that he left for work at 9:30 in the morning, dashed home for supper at 8, and went back to the store until the last customer left, which in those early days could be 11 o'clock or later.

Tom and Betsy quickly blended. They were married August 27, 1949, and moved into a little house on 29th Street in Moline.

"Honey, this is going to be a challenging life for you."

"We had so little furniture, we sat on beer cases," Tom says.

They had six children. For years, young Paul thought Dad took a vacation during the month of December. They never saw him, because that was the month he was shepherding the assembly of thousands of fruit baskets at the store.

Betsy never quite left the store. As the children grew older, she was back at the sandwich board.

And her husband was right there, running the Moline store and putting the pickle on the plates.

Betsy made the sandwiches ... egg salad, ham and cheese, corned beef on homemade rye.

Tom always had the same thing to say, "I'll pickle your plate."

It made the diners laugh.

15

The fruit basket bonanza
"It may look like a warehouse, but we call it atmosphere"

Those were the golden days …

It is the week or two before Christmas. Lagomarcino's in Moline is organized chaos. The store is closed to customers because all the space is jam-packed, every square foot needed to make giant fruit baskets.

The tile floor is squishy with grapes. The whole place has the fruity essence of a market place in Rome. Cases of fresh fruit are stacked 10-high.

Tom Sr. is trying his best to appear calm. If a customer squeezes in, he says, "It may look like a warehouse, but we call it atmosphere."

Lagomarcino's would turn out 200 fruit baskets a day.

Tom finds calm in joking. He tells a customer, "It's so busy today that we brought the dog down from upstairs to lick the labels."

They are golden labels — like shiny coins — for the baskets that will be hand-delivered to each recipient. Businesses have ordered Lago fruit baskets by the dozen for their choice customers.

The soda fountain counter is an assembly line. Lagomarcino fruit baskets are so coveted that at least 2,000 of them will be assembled in a Christmas season.

They are hand-created artistic marvels. Family members are finicky. Only the best can go into their baskets … Golden Delicious apples and Washington Reds; greenish-yellow Anjou and fair-shaded Bartlett pears; and the biggest oranges on the market. Tom is fussy about oranges. Only 64's, 72's and 88's are allowed. The numbers represent the size of oranges — 64's being the biggest, almost the size of grapefruits. Each number tells how many are packed in a case.

Once, during the week before Christmas, a Catholic priest wanders into the store. He is puzzled by the mayhem of all that fruit, and how so many

"It's so busy today that we brought the dog down from upstairs to lick the labels."

people are making baskets.

"Allow me to help," the sympathetic priest says, working a full shift. "Every one of those 200 or so baskets that went out that day were blessed by a priest," Tom says.

Delivery is a nightmare. Some people will come to the store for their basket. There are name tags but, as it happens, they can get mixed up. Most baskets are the same, so Tom hands them someone else's basket.

"Sometimes we have to rob Peter to pay Paul," he says.

Tom recalls a holiday season from his youth: "Wow, I found out that I was delivering baskets in a red light district. The address was upstairs and the young woman was showing all her assets. She said to me, 'Oh, honey, put the basket on the table and come on over here.' It scared the hell out of me. I got out of there fast."

It is difficult to move in the store because the bananas, which are in gigantic, heavy boxes, cover the milk glass-topped tables of the booths.

No one fusses or argues in this pocket of fruity stress. But there are differences of opinion. Uncle Joe likes to put tangerines in the baskets because they don't roll off the round oranges. Tom resists. Italian words stream. Italian is spoken only during disagreements. Tom tells Uncle Joe: "Tangerines look like oranges that lost their air."

So, Uncle Joe returns to the baskets. No basket will leave the store without his distinctive touch. He carefully fashions a big cluster of red grapes on the very top.

"Christmas season was wild," says Tom Jr. "I would be on the phone all day, taking orders, answering with the greeting 'Lagomarcino's.' One Christmas Eve, the whole family — totally exhausted — went to midnight Mass. We were taking Communion, and when the priest said 'Body of Christ,' I was so used to saying the family name over the phone that I said, 'Lagomarcino's' instead of 'Amen.'

"I was afraid I was going to get a call from the Pope."

The sweet chaos of holidays

Holidays are too much for anyone to lightly wish upon anyone else. Hordes of people crowd into the two Lagomarcino stores with a solitary thing in mind — candy! They are happy shoppers. They are not pushy, picking and choosing and waiting their turn at the cash registers.

Candy is happiness.

At Christmas time, the Lago stores will make 4,000 pounds of homemade chocolates. That is 2 tons! They sell so many chocolates that sometimes the supply runs out and a batch has to be made on Christmas Eve.

"We can handle anything; we just work harder," says Tom Jr. "Christmas can be like a herd of cattle wanting candy."

"Christmas can be like a herd of cattle wanting candy."

The Moline store is long and narrow. If someone calls out for Tom Sr., he might be heard to reply, "I'm down in the basement, holding up the floor." There can be that many people!

No one acts impatient, but Tom Sr. works the crowd: "Stick around for the floor show." He says store workers are so busy that they are tired before getting to work.

Christmas can get out of hand at the Moline store, where 200 fruit baskets a day have been assembled and at least 2,000 hand-delivered. No food can be served; the counters and booths are filled with baskets. Windows are fruit and candy, pyramids of oranges and candy.

"Christmas is always the biggest season," says Tom Jr. "We always make a 4-foot-tall, 35-pound chocolate Santa. One year, sweet Santa was too close to some spotlights and began to melt. He lost his balance and took a nose dive. It just missed Jean Schebler of Davenport."

Easter is the second-biggest season. One year, Lago's shipped 8,000 of those famous chocolate eggs filled with wrapped milk chocolates.

Traditions, too: The Lago eggs have become nostalgic memories in chocolate. Says Angela Florence of Rock Island: "When I cracked open my first Lagomarcino Easter egg as a 20-something newlywed, it was like being a kid all over again. My husband's family introduced me to one of their favorite Lago traditions."

Valentine's Day is No. 3 in the chaotic Lago life. The Moline store windows are decorated with hearts and streamers and chocolates until they look like a Rose Bowl float.

Says Lisa Lagomarcino Ambrose: "We will dip 2,000 fresh strawberries, in dark and milk chocolate, for Valentine's Day."

During the bedlam of such days, Tom Sr. — in white apron — has been seen to rush around telling everyone, "Great day! Great day! Everything's all right. It just looks bad."

The finest and largest selection of Heart Boxes in the quad cities......

PACKED WITH HOME MADE

Lagomarcino's Chocolates

BEAUTIFUL BOXES
All Sizes
All Prices

When a guy's in love — or in trouble

There always has to be a biggest something or other, and the biggest box of Lagomarcino chocolates regularly assembled is the Harem. It was named by Betsy Lagomarcino, wife of Tom Sr., who is shown with the calorie-laden load.

Contents: 300 pieces of chocolates
Weight: 7 to 8 pounds
Time it takes to pack: At least 1½ hours
Price: $199

Purchasers are always men. Usually triggered by how much in love a guy is, or how much he is in the dog house.

It is not a big-selling item, but as many as seven Harem Specials are sold each year, during Valentine season.

The finest and largest selection of Heart Boxes in the quad cities......

PACKED WITH HOME MADE
Lagomarcino's Chocolates

BEAUTIFUL BOXES
All Sizes
All Prices

A man named Gilbert

He was a young romantic who believed that his wife deserved the best and fanciest. Every year, Gilbert bought his wife a special Valentine box of chocolates at Lagomarcino's in Moline. They were always elaborate boxes, which she saved. Gilbert would come in every year to study the new boxes, and then return home to examine the old boxes his wife had saved. Back and forth he studied boxes in the fussy Valentine window display and at home. After lord-only-knows how many trips, he would make a choice of the just-right box and have it packed with his wife's favorites — coconut clusters, cordial cherries, sponge candy and white pretzels.

Isn't it romantic?

Warm hands and a cold soda

"Forget love … I'd rather fall in chocolate," a quipster once said. That's not how it went for Sue and Howard Petersen of Los Angeles, Calif. She tells it this way:

"We were students at Moline High and met at Lago's. I can't say that it was love at first sight, but a chocolate soda broke the ice. We split a chocolate soda. I was kind of nervous and held onto the glass quite awhile. That made my hands cold. I told Howard, 'My hands are cold.' He told me to hold his, which were very warm. That's all that was needed, holding hands over a chocolate soda. We finished high school and college and have been married for 30 years."

A sparkler in a chocolate egg

Beth Lagomarcino was edgy when a diamond ring sent from Florida arrived at the Moline store. The diamond was intended to be a romantic treat inside one of those 2,000 colossal eggs that Beth and others were making and shipping all over the world for Easter. "I had heard way down here in Florida of your chocolate eggs and their rough exterior," wrote the romantic guy. He wanted to propose marriage by way of a chocolate egg.

"Please wrap the ring in some distinctive manner so that she can tell that it is different from the rest of the candy treats inside. Romance lives in us all, and the chocolate sweetens the journey while nourishing the soul."

He asked that a simple card be placed with the ring inside the egg:

Linda —
Will you marry me?
John

Beth says the egg arrived intact and that Linda accepted John's sweet proposal.

Courting over lunch

"Twenty-five years ago, my future husband, John, and I met regularly at the Moline Lago's for a romantic lunch in one of the center booths. We were courting over our respective liverwurst and corned beef sandwiches and vanilla sodas. How my heart pounded as I sat across the table from my true love!"
— *Nancy Hayes, Davenport, Iowa*

Walk home was worth the trip

"In 1940, during my freshman year at St. Mary's High School in Moline, I invited a cute little girl, a classmate, to have a Coke with me after school at Lago's. We really enjoyed it, but I didn't tell her the money I spent was my bus fare. I had to walk home — and I lived a mile beyond the last stop in Silvis."
— *Paul R. Vyncke, East Moline, Illinois*

Love was in the air

"On July 7, 2007 — nerve-riddled — I got down on one knee at the Moline store and asked my beautiful Johnna to marry me. She said "yes," and now we will have the everlasting memory that it all happened at Lago's."
— *Jefferson B.T. Jackson, Rock Island, Illinois*

The initials on the mirror

"Many years ago (61), a very young boy, Carl Freeman, met Betty Schatteman at the skating rink in Moline and began dating. Of course, young people need to have their place to sit and talk for awhile, so they chose Lago's. On one of those stops, the young man asked the girl to marry him and she said, 'Yes' and he gave her a diamond engagement ring.

"Young people like to leave a message of their love. There was no tree to carve their initials on, so they left them on a mirror in the booth in the left side of the store. As time went by, they would occasionally visit their personal booth. A year later, they were married. We don't know if BJS X CF are still in that booth, but it is our personal love story."
— *Betty and Carl Freeman Jr., East Moline, Illinois*

(The rest of the story: The initials are gone. The mirror was long ago replaced. But the love remains.)

The 25-cent date

Love and marriage go together like whipped cream on top of a Lago's sundae. "My parents were engaged in the early 1940s," says Steve Walker of Bettendorf, Iowa. "On that evening, my dad had 25 cents in his pocket. To celebrate their engagement, my parents took the street car for a dime to Lago's and split a soda for 15 cents to celebrate their special day. They walked home."

Another first date

"My late husband, Carl 'Boots' Aronson, and I came to Lago's in 1951 on our first date after we had been to the movies. We must have had a hot chocolate or hot fudge sundae, and we came back many times on our anniversary."
— *Alice Aronson, Rock Island, Illinois*

Valentine goes in the dog house

Dad brought his three little sons into a Lago store to pick out a Valentine heart for Mom. There was a lot of thought going into this. They were overwhelmed by all the bright red hearts filled with candy. After much deliberation, they decided on just the right one and had it filled with her favorite chocolates.

Dad turned to the boys and said: "Now, where are we going to hide this heart?"

The oldest boy said, "We can hide it in my room."

The second boy said, "No way! You will eat it!"

The youngest boy yelled, "I know! We can put it in the dog house. Mom will never go in there."

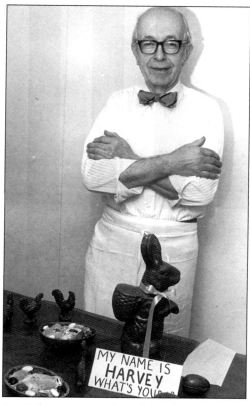

Joe Schenone, candymaker, always a bow tie and some of his favorite chocolate pets.

Harvey the rabbit

Harvey is not a hippity-hop rabbit. He just perches there, in chocolate stance. He is too cute to eat, but that is his destiny.

Each Easter season, Lagomarcino's casts several "Harveys" in chocolate. Each Harvey weighs somewhere between 9 and 13 pounds. They are semi-solid. If solid, a Harvey would almost be too heavy to lift.

Harveys sell for $175, and every Easter a few find a home.

A few years ago, one daddy bought a Harvey for each of his three daughters.

"It took several days of courage for the girls to begin to nibble on their Harveys," Dad says.

Once, when Easter was late in the spring season, the weather turned warm. It was hot in the window of the Moline store. Harvey began to melt. Before the day was over, he didn't look much like a rabbit. He resembled the Wicked Witch of the West.

The sweet taste of autumn on a stick

God makes the apples, but Lagomarcino's gives them a luscious, russet coat of caramel. Never call a Lago's apple a taffy apple. Lago apples are caramel apples.

From mid-September through October, Lago's will dip at least 8,000 apples. It is hand work, with the caramel gently heated in a mammoth copper kettle.

Gala apples are used because they dip best and show a shiny glow when teeth are gnashed through the soft caramel into the apple. The caramel recipe is a secret; one hush-hush ingredient is heavy whipping cream.

Mostly, you think of caramel apples as an autumn treat. In fact, as Joe Taylor of Hampton, Illinois, says: "I know fall has arrived when the 'Caramel Apples' sign goes out in front of the store."

But their appeal reaches in many directions. "We have made them for bar mitzvahs and weddings," says Lisa Lagomarcino Ambrose.

Caramel apples lined up alongside wedding cakes for guests to grab? A tricky balance …

There are requests for caramel apples all year around, but they are made only in autumn for an obvious reason: Gala apples are at their best in the fall.

"No," the man replied. "I'm calling from Iraq."

This is a starter for a quite blissful Easter story, the first of this season. It has an O. Henry twist.

Deb continued the phone conversation, the voice at the other end sounding hollow, like it was coming from the bottom of an oak barrel.

"I want to order one of your big chocolate eggs for my wife," the caller said. "You know, those great big ones. And I want three of the smaller ones for my daughters."

Deb leaned hard into the phone to get all the details.

"You want one of those big guys, the $68.95 eggs that are filled with candy?"

"That's it," he replied. "Do you take a credit card from Iraq?"

"Of course."

It came to be that the caller was 1st Sgt. Scott Wolf of Stockton, a pocket-size town of about 200 folks out west of Davenport. He knew of those big eggs — and who doesn't? They've been a feature in Saveur, one of the most uppity of gourmet magazines.

For his wife, Christine, he wanted a big chocolate egg, the one that is like getting a box of chocolates and being able to eat the box, too. Along with the big egg, which is larger than a football, he ordered smaller versions for his daughters, Whitney, 9; Autumn, 6; and Heidi, 3. It was to be kept a secret. He wanted his family to be surprised that he would be thinking of them from a place of war.

Well, that was that. Deb took all the details and assured Scott the eggs would be delivered in time for Easter. It was to be a surprise. But that surprise was not to last very long.

"Within 15 minutes of my talking to that man in Iraq, a woman came to the counter to order some candy," Deb says. "I noticed that she was wearing a big pin with a picture of a serviceman. I told her that I had just talked to a soldier in Iraq, and he had ordered one of our big chocolate eggs for his wife.

The customer casually asked where the military man was from.

"Stockton, Iowa," answered Deb.

"What was his name?"

"First Sgt. Scott Wolf."

The customer was shocked. She pointed to her pin with the serviceman's picture. "That's my husband, Scott."

It was a one-in-a-couple-million chance that all this would happen, but now the secret was out. They were ordering eggs for each other.

Scott, who works at Alcoa Davenport Works, is attached to the 224th Engineering Battalion. He was called to duty with the National Guard and has been overseas for three months. He expects 18 months of duty in Iraq.

"He tells me that he isn't in a dangerous area, but they recently lost two guys from his outfit," his wife says.

She is thrilled that her husband would remember the family tradition. "It began in 1991. It will be five years this Easter that he began giving me a big chocolate egg."

At Lagomarcino's, they're assured the big milk chocolate egg and the three little ones will be at the Wolf home for Easter.

"If we can ship one of our eggs to Budapest — which we are doing right now — I think we can get four delivered to Stockton," says Tom Lagomarcino, the chief of sweets, "and another delivered to Iraq."

The rest of the story ...

So many times, we depend on the kindness of strangers. Last Sunday, we told about a soldier in Iraq calling Lagomarcino's and ordering a football-size chocolate Easter egg for his wife in Stockton. He wanted three smaller chocolate eggs for his daughters.

The morning after the column appeared, a woman came to Lago's in the Village of East Davenport and said, "I want to pay for those eggs."

That amounted to about $100, and Lago's obliged by canceling the credit card charge that the sergeant had made.

Says Tom Lagomarcino Jr.: "A half-dozen others have wanted to pay for the eggs, but we told them that this anonymous woman had first dibs on paying. We've been touched by the kindness of people wanting to pay for the eggs."

Old lovers, and always a date on the 14th

Paul and Mia Morgan met in Romania during the burning days of World War II.

"It was miserable, tragic, but we were in love, and so were married," Mia used to say.

Some time after the war, they made it to America and found their way to Davenport, not far from Lagomarcino's Village of East Davenport store, where they were regular customers. Employees came to be devoted to them.

"There was love in their eyes," Lisa Lagomarcino Ambrose says of the couple who always sat in a booth along the wall. He would pat her hand.

Mia was a tiny, sparrow-like woman; Paul was more husky.

Paul and Mia never failed to have lunch at Lago's on the 14th day of each month. They could be depended on to sit in the same booth.

They never said why the 14th was a magic day. In truth it was the day they became engaged. Once — not on the 14th— the aging couple appeared, and she whispered that it was her birthday. Lago's hurriedly assembled a cake.

On the 14th, of each month, there was no need ask their choice for lunch. Mia would order a double chocolate soda.

Paul had a heftier appetite, a ham salad sandwich on rye, potato salad, a tomato salad and double chocolate pecan sundae with whipped cream.

Explicitly, he would warn: "But no bananas." He had his own way of pronouncing it, "bah-nah-nas."

The ritual of the 14th continued for years. Mia, who was in her 80s, grew weaker and slower of step while he held the door for her. One day, she died. People at Lago's wondered if the 14th luncheon would continue.

It did, for years. Always, Paul was there on the 14th, lonely in the booth, but ordering the same menu, emphasizing no "bah-nah-nas." One 14th, though, he did not appear. Employees were heartbroken to learn that he had died.

Lisa says, "They never fell out of love."

Smo-o-o-o-oth
The magic of a malt or shake

Once upon a time, on a Saturday before Easter Sunday, a little girl sat with her mom and grandmother in a booth at Lagomarcino's in Moline. She carried her little purse and was determined to personally pay for her order. She was insistent, as only a 5-year-old can be, on what she wanted.

"A *strawbunny* milk shake," she said.

Not a chocolate milk shake, or a chocolate malt, or a strawberry shake. A strawbunny shake.

"This is a new one," a soda jerk said, so the inventive fountain crew created the first strawbunny milk shake.

For that strawbunny shake, a marshmallow was split to make ears. A lump of vanilla ice cream was the head. Chocolate chips were the eyes and a maraschino cherry was the bright red nose.

"There is only one way to make a malt or a shake," says Tom Jr. "It's the old-fashioned way, and that is to make them smooth."

The customer picks out the flavor — maybe one with real strawberries, or chocolate. Into a tall metal container called a can goes squirts of flavor, or the fruit. Then, three scoops of vanilla ice cream, followed by a little milk. The can is clamped to a Hamilton Beach mixer.

Whirr, buzz. The mixed magic is poured into a tall glass — never a wax-coated paper cup. There is always too much, so the customer is given the remainder, still in the can — always steamy cold, with driplets of dampness running down the sides.

The only difference between a malted milk and a milk shake is malted milk powder. Otherwise, it's the same multi-calorie gratification.

"First time I came to Lago's was in the spring of 1958 with my buddies after a Little League baseball game," recalls Terry Dove of Clarendon, Texas. "I had my first chocolate malt. I was hooked."

A Lago's shake is a cross-generational thing. As Kelly Jean Ingold of Milan says, "Ever since I was very young, my grandmother and I would have 'Grams and Granddaughter' days. Lunch at Lago's was always a must. Although my grandmother has passed away, to this day I order the same exact thing — grilled cheese with a good old chocolate shake."

51

BUILDING THE PERFECT SODA

Lagomarcino's | Since 1908

The fine art of making a soda

To be called a soda jerk is a respected title, because there is an art to making a soda.

At some cutesy or quickie places, it may be called a "float." That is sacrilege, when compared to a real soda.

To make a soda is a craft.

A soda must be served in a tall glass, with a striped straw and long silver spoon. Never in a paper or plastic cup.

A professional soda jerk takes the glass firmly in hand and squirts in two or three shots of syrup. A single spoon of vanilla ice cream goes in next.

Lisa and Carol Lagomarcino sip on a soda.

In the bottom of the glass, the syrup and ice cream are mulled together. This is followed by a fine stream of carbonated soda water.

It now becomes delicate, and finesse is important. The stream of carbonated water must fill only two-thirds of the glass. Then, two scoops of vanilla ice cream are carefully dropped into the glass. The soda is finished off with another stream of carbonated soda water that embellishes the soda with a nice, foamy head.

"It's creamy; you can taste the difference in a real soda," says Lisa Lagomarcino Ambrose, who has been a soda jerk since childhood.

Mamata Marme of DeWitt, Iowa, says, "My niece was here on a trip from India. She had a double chocolate soda for lunch, and another for dessert. She came back six years later and her first request was a trip to Lagomarcino's ... for a soda."

The memories of Jackie Shattuck, 68 years old, of Coal Valley, Illinois, are long and sweet: "When I was in nurses' training at Moline Public Hospital, we gals would skip down the hill to Lago's for ice cream sodas. They are to die for!"

53

Sweet Memories   Bill Wundram

Uncle Joe scrapes soft warm brittle from the kettle.

Carefully, he thins it out on a marble table.

As a master candy maker, he flips the peanut brittle to cool.

Peanut Brittle

Autumn's favorite crunch

It starts with a big copper kettle — the biggest owned by Lagomarcino's — and from there on, making peanut brittle is tricky. Peanut brittle arrives with the season of jack-o-lanterns, and leaves us before springtime. It all depends on the weather. Peanut brittle doesn't like warm weather.

It is best made in small batches. The candy maker must keep a close eye on that kettle. The fussy peanut brittle chef must make certain that the sugars and other ingredients are cooked to a golden brown. Good grief, the worst is to allow it to burn! Caramelized, it is spread as a thin sheet onto marble, cooled, then cut into three sections and carefully turned. Next, it is stretched by hand to get a thin, translucent peanut brittle.

On days when peanut brittle is made, the essence of a Lago store is the sweet smell of peanuts. It is the crunchy soul of Indian summer.

55

Life is a cup
of hot chocolate ...

"Love is like drinking hot chocolate before it has cooled off. It takes you by surprise at first, but keeps you warm for a long time."

A group of graduates, well established in their careers, were talking at a reunion and decided to visit their old university professor, now retired. During their visit, the conversation turned to complaints about stress in their work and lives. Offering his guests hot chocolate, the professor went into the kitchen and returned with a large pot of hot chocolate and an assortment of cups — porcelain, glass, crystal, some plain looking, some expensive, some exquisite.

When they each had a cup of hot chocolate in hand, the professor said: "Notice that all the nice-looking, expensive cups were taken, leaving behind the plain and cheap ones. While it is normal for you to want only the best for yourselves, that is the source of your problems and stress. The cup that you're drinking from adds nothing to the quality of the hot chocolate. In most cases it is just more expensive and in some cases even hides what we drink. What all of you really wanted was hot chocolate, not the cup; but you consciously went for the best cups ... And then you began eyeing each other's cups.

"After the Festival of Trees parade, we always come into the hustle and bustle of Lago's to get a steaming mug of chocolate "deliciousness" and a cup of soup and a hearty ham salad sandwich. We always end with a great big toddler smile at the candy counter."

Lindsay and Maddelin Meeker, Davenport

"Now, consider this: Life is the hot chocolate; your job, money and position in society are the cups. They are just tools to hold and contain life. The cup you have does not define, nor change the quality of life you have. Sometimes, by concentrating only on the cup, we fail to enjoy the hot chocolate God has provided us. God makes the hot chocolate; we people choose the cups.

"The happiest people don't have the best of everything. They just make the best of everything that they have.

"Live simply. Love generously. Care deeply. Speak kindly. And enjoy your hot chocolate."

(Source unknown)

The holiness of chocolate

There had been a death in the family, or difficulty of some sort, so the two women — rolling and dipping Lagomarcino chocolates — were distraught. They could not go through such sad moments without the comforts of the rosary, so chocolates became a holy object.

Elisa Pizano suggested to Anita Schenone that, as they rolled and dipped and prayed together, they should substitute each vanilla cream for a rosary bead and a Hail Mary.

It reminded, in a way, of the memorable TV scene of Lucille Ball and Vivian Vance on the assembly line at the chocolate factory. Elisa, with sparkling eyes and bubbly personality, was the talkative one. Anita was just learning English in place of her native Italian.

Anita Schenone – once, chocolates became rosary beads.

Elisa taught Anita a lot of English, but Anita learned a lot from watching TV. She would sometimes get confused.

For an exclamation of surprise, she would burst out with, "From the land of sky blue waters!" Of course, being Italian, she would often accentuate her points by waving a chocolate covered hand.

Lost in candy land

Customers stand in a daze. Some are immobilized in awe. Eyes are glazed. Is this heaven? Jaws drop. The bulk candy cases at Lagomarcino's stores are rainbows of sugared lemon drops and watermelon slices, 2-foot-long gummi snakes and syrup-filled wax bottles.

There may be bigger assortments of bulk candy in this land, but where? Customers come from afar — all over the Midwest — to buy candy at Lago's.

One customer drives from Oak Park, Illinois, near Chicago, to buy candy for her bridge club. She has done this for 35 years.

It used to be called penny candy; now, it is more exotica. Stroll along in candy land; all the favorites are lusciously there, some in tall jars that shine like Waterford crystal.

"I remember having my Dad hold me up so I could see the candy and chocolates in the window cases."
Joline (Theis) Scott
East Moline, Illinois

There are white Jordan almonds, essential for Greek and Italian weddings, and butterscotch buttons, peppermint starlights and rock candy. That rock candy is a store staple, crystallized clear sugar on a string.

Eyes dream along the rows of trays and jars; the candies are so colorful that sunglasses are needed. Dozens and dozens of sweets, like Swedish fish and Holland mints. Galactic jaw breakers, big as a baby's fist, look too large to fit in even a giant's mouth. Kids still love the syrup-filled wax bottles, the old-fashioned kind that grandma and grandpa bought. There are raspberries and blackberries and smooth and melty mints. Always, the gummis — gummi clowns, frogs, bears, cherries and sharks. And neon crawlers, which the kids call sour worms, and sour flip-flops. Mississippi river rocks are really chocolate hunks.

"I'll take some of these, and some of those ..."

Saltwater taffy is a much-loved summer favorite; double-dipped malted milk balls are popular all year long. There is a tray of red and black licorice wheels. Licorice has always been big at Lago's, treats like licorice pipes, red and black, and twisted strands of red, black and chocolate licorice. Licorice lovers can't get enough black jelly beans.

Once, Aunt Mary Lagomarcino was waiting on a man who wanted black jelly beans. She giggled when he ordered, "A pound of jack belly beans."

Customers cannot control themselves at the shiny glass counters. "I'll take some of these, and some of those" … cherry sours, fruit slices, chocolate bridge mix and chocolate espresso beans — chocolate-covered coffee beans.

Candy comes in novelties at Lago's, like chocolate gold coins, candy necklaces, chocolate cars and chocolate lady bugs. It's nostalgia land. Lago's still has candy dots on paper.

"I still get inquiries for French creams, and cream filberts that we called mothballs, and licorice buttons," says Beth Lagomarcino. There are two jars for anise squares, the most popular hard candy, and root beer barrels.

"People can't find anise candy anywhere else but at Lagomarcino's," she smiles.

In so many sweet words, if you can't find it at Lago's, you likely can't find it anywhere.

In honor of the 100th anniversary, Tom Roberts recreated the back bar for the Moline store. The bar was designed by Judith Malone, built by Roberts, with stained glass work by John Watts.

The stores
Frozen in time, but with a candy box floor

Once, women were not allowed to sit on the little round stools at the soda fountain in the Moline Lagomarcino's. It would have been improper to have their derrieres possibly hang over the sides.

Call them frozen in time, but Lagomarcino's stores Moline and Davenport are treasures in Americana. Call it ambience, call it mood, but the uniqueness is there — including the round stools at the soda fountain.

64

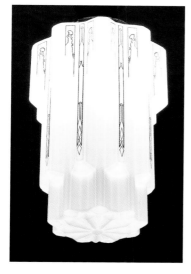

Come in and be cozy, the stores seem to say. You'll feel a calmness, a satisfying wistfulness as memories drift quietly past your table or booth.

Even the floors are homespun.

The original 1908 Cassini terrazo tile floor at the Moline store is intact. The floor of the 1997 Village of East Davenport store is tile, too, but with a 21st-century twist. The tile colors are a maze, a speckle of non-patterns. The floor was designed to look like the inside of a candy box.

In 1921, the old Moline Furniture Works built the booths for the Moline store. A couple generations later, a granddaughter of one of the owners of the furniture works received a marriage proposal in one of grandpa's booths. She said yes.

Look closely at the booth sides. Raised in the wood is the pattern of a soda fountain glass.

Leaded glass tulip lights, made in 1921 for the Moline store, are reproduced in the Davenport store.

The Bastian & Blessing dispensers, with knobs and necks that look like giraffes, are identical in each place. Davenport's soda fountain came from Crawfordsville, Indiana, in 1940. The Davenport back bar is from the old Snow White Pharmacy in Maquoketa, Iowa.

The Lagomarcino clan is finicky about authenticity. New walnut booths had to be built for Davenport, just like

Moline's. One month after another passed while cabinet makers fussed and trimmed. The Lagomarcinos were impatient.

"You won't get the booths until God says they're ready," said one of the cabinet makers, Butch Carver.

Tom Jr. told him, "I just talked to God, and he says they're ready."

The booths were lovely and shiny when installed, but too snug a fit. Before the Village store opened, 6 inches was cut off the end of the booth tables, and no one has known the difference. Now, they're comfy. The booths match all the walnut cabinets in the place.

The round stools at the fountain twirl, as of old, which reminds of the day when a little girl came in with her grandma. Grammy chose a table. The granddaughter said, "No, we have to sit at the counter; that's where the action is."

Reluctantly, Grandma sat on one of the stools. For safety's sake, employees came up with a belt to secure grandma to the stool.

How Lago's got a chocolate sweet tooth

Always, Lagomarcino's sold candy. But in the beginning, candy was unimportant. There were hard horehound drops and rock candy, anise and candy canes. More important to the store was the fruit, long bunches of bananas hanging in the front windows and pyramids of California Sunkist oranges.

There was the cigar counter, too, where Lago's did a lively business in Brown Beauty cigars, Fatima and Lucky Strike cigarettes and Copenhagen snuff in flat little cans. Tobacco was big, with a gas lighter on a tall stick for the sports to light their stogies,

Once, candy was a trifling ring of the cash register, but Tom Sr. and his brother Charlie — always the entrepreneurs — eyed chocolate in their future.

Chocolate became the sweet foundation of the business.

It wouldn't have been that way without the name of Meadowbrook, which is almost forgotten in the heavens of candy land.

Moline Candy Manufacturing Co. claimed to make the world's best vanilla creams.

"They did," says Tom Sr. "It was a delicious product."

The company had a retail store in downtown Moline called the Sugar Bowl, but there was a shift of owners and company names. When it became Meadowbrook Candy Co., it hit the national market.

"They were very big, with recipes that made us envious," says Tom Sr. "We saw a future in candy, and 70 years ago (1938) my brother bought the company, the equipment and the recipes."

Many of the old Meadowbrook chocolates recipes are still the same ones used today by the Lagomarcino chocolatiers.

There's a long, big sign in the Moline Lagomarcino's. It says "Meadowbrook" — homage to the great-grandfather of the Lago line of chocolates.

Sweet Memories   Bill Wundram

Presto, chango

The magic of making sponge candy

Sponge candy is mysteriously sweet, highly sensitive to heat and humidity. It can disappear — and not just into your mouth.

It is a hocus-pocus concoction that almost vanishes from a hunk of sweetness into a soft liquid-like sponge if the weather is hot.

Lago's is one of the few places in America that makes authentic sponge candy. For Ed Connelly of Bettendorf, that was a selling point when he was courting his wife. "My wife grew up in Colorado and thought it was the only place she could find sponge candy. On our second or third date, we went to Lagomarcino's. Now, she gets sponge candy on her birthday and on Valentine's Day."

At first bite, sponge candy is crisp. Then, it melts in your mouth. It is covered in dark or milk chocolate, and tastes like molasses and caramelized sugar.

The first ingredients go into a giant copper kettle and are heated for an

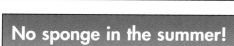

hour. The kettle is taken from the heat and allowed to slightly cool. Final ingredients are added and, in a few minutes — presto, chango — the sponge begins to double and redouble in size until it fills the kettle. For those who sneak a peek at the process, it is mind-boggling.

Next, the sponge is poured onto an antique marble table where it will cool for hours before being cut by hand, with a sharp knife, into pieces.

There is nationwide demand for Lagomarcino's sponge candy. It can be made only in cooler months.

"It's frantic to keep up with the demand between October and early June," says Tom Sr.

It's frantic — and it's tradition for many families. "My grandmother, Elsie Bennington, always had sponge candy from Lago's as a special treat," recalls Bekky Anderson of Davenport. "When she passed on, my mother, Opal Gellerstedt, continued the tradition. Today, I continue the tradition of sponge candy at Christmas."

No sponge in the summer!

One day, Tom Jr. was talking about candy at the Hampton (Illinois) Public Library with a group of 6- and 7-year-olds.

It was 95 degrees, and the kids were rambunctious. One lad was particularly active, jumping around the place. To calm him down, Tom gave him a hunk of sponge candy and asked him to put it outside in a pie tin. The boy was to sit quietly until given the signal to bring it back inside.

The little boy ran back into the library, nearly speechless.

"It's all gone," he exclaimed.

All that was left was — in the child's words — "a glob of goo."

A lesson had been learned.

No sponge candy in the summer.

Apricot

Caramel

Butter

Strawberry

Cher

Caramel
Peanut
Cluster

Black
Walnut

Vanilla

Raspberr

he code

Chocolate

Orange

English Toffee

Pineapple

trawberry

Chocolate

Coconut

Maple

Vanilla

Breaking the box of chocolates code

*… or, how to decipher
all those artistic squiggles*

Chocolate is the best when it melts so creamy and soft in your mouth and it slides down your throat.

But …

The nagging, delicious question — when you get a box of chocolates — is what's inside those luscious-looking bon-bons. There is always that risk that you might end up with vanilla when you wanted strawberry.

The secret is in the chocolate penmanship. Those mystic marks, the swirls and whirls, are exacting, cursive, Spencerian penmanship that will reveal what's inside the chocolates.

In the word of professional chocolatiers, it is called stringing. It takes a trained professional to be a stringer. Lagomarcino's has a string of stringers, or chocolate penmanship professionals.

To watch them work is remarkable. First comes the cream or fondant that goes inside. It is mixed in a copper kettle, stirred with a wooden paddle. The creams are rolled, and then come the chocolate covering and the stringing.

In one swoop, the candy dippers "string." That is, they create — as if writing — an initial on the warm piece of chocolate. With a twist of the wrist, a cursive letter is made. Sometimes they use a pointer finger or a pinkie to fully finesse the whirl.

Stringers string in code. A "V" on top of a chocolate means the inside is vanilla. An "M" is for maple. "R" for raspberry. "B" for buttercream. "S" for strawberry. A straight line means coconut. "P" means pineapple. A double loop is for black walnut. A big loop stands for chocolate.

"Life is like a box of chocolates. You never know what you're gonna get."
— Forrest Gump,
in the movie
"Forrest Gump"

The finest chocolate has a low melting point. It should melt with the touch of a finger and that's why people with cold hands under their plastic gloves are the best stringers, or dippers. Lagomarcino dippers don't use thermometers because they can feel the velvety smoothness.

Making chocolates is tedious work. For many years, the peanuts were individually dipped in chocolate for peanut clusters. A dipper named Henrietta became so weary of dipping peanuts one by one that she threatened to quit. The Lago family relented. They allowed her to dip them in bunches.

Working with chocolate is like a tender love affair.

"Chocolate has to be handled carefully," says Tom Sr. "Too much heat takes it out of temper, separating the cocoa butter and the chocolate."

Tom Sr. has a love affair with chocolate, which is 60 percent of the Lago business.

He says, "Chocolate revives my senses. I think chocolate even in the middle of the night."

Fun and more fun
at the soda fountain

"The only thing better than fun is more fun"

There was the day when two elephants tried to nudge their way through the front door of Lagomarcino's in Moline … and the time a bunch of long-haired Mongolians pounded on the locked door of the place … and jams of people on the night that Neil Diamond played the grand opening of The Mark of the Quad-Cities, now the i wireless Center.

It didn't make any difference that Neil wasn't inside the store; customers just wanted to eat one of the Neil Diamond sundaes the store was selling that night.

A Lagomarcino store can be a wild and crazy place. It can be holy-like, too, on nights like the annual Candlelight Christmas concerts, when high school choirs sing at the Village of East Davenport store.

There was the time when a 15-piece band from Germany settled down for lunch at the Village place. They serenaded, oompa-pa-pa. When Cara Lagomarcino brought their food, she was frantically confused. "They all look alike," she said. "They're all in lederhosen."

Another day, a couple dozen French students showed up for sundaes. Not one could speak English.

"There are lots of crazy moments in our places," says Tom Jr.

There was noontime bedlam when a big limo pulled up with actress Brooke Shields. She ordered a tuna salad on homemade rye and a strawberry sundae. The buzz spread around downtown Moline that the star was at Lago's.

"The place was a long line of people buying a package of gum, just to get a look at the star," says Tom Jr.

One customer asked, "Which one is Brooke?"

Tom Sr., smiling like the Cheshire cat, said: "She's the gorgeous one in the third booth." He tightened his necktie and said, "She came in here to see me."

A typical summer afternoon, a group of women might be playing bridge in the Village of East Davenport store. Bridge at Lago's is a social event.

On a Sunday, a bunch of Mongolians — in town with the circus — came pounding at the locked door of the Moline store. They were angry, shouting that they were hungry. "We weren't going to turn down that gang" says Tom Jr. "They just about ate us out of food."

Two elephants from the circus loped to the store one noon. With their trunks they sniffed at the front door.

"To prove that we could handle any appetite," says Beth Lagomarcino, "we gave them 40 loaves of bread."

One of their keepers ordered a butterscotch sundae.

"But no nuts," he said. "One of those elephants swatted me with his trunk last week and knocked out my front teeth."

As Tom Sr. likes to say, "The only thing better than fun is more fun."

77

I scream, you scream …
we all scream for ice cream

There is no more soul-stirring surprise than the first adventure with ice cream. It is a great equalizer. No one can have a sour face when they're eating Lagomarcino's ice cream.

H.C. Duke & Son, a manufacturer of ice cream manufacturing equipment, ran an advertisement in a trade magazine:

"It's not our grandfather's ice cream machine.
But wait a minute, it is …"

The ad was talking about Lago's, which has had only two ice cream machines in its 100-year life.

For years, Tom Sr. would moan: "I'm chained to the ice cream machine." He turned it out in front of the customers, not far from the soda fountain in the center of the Moline store. He wanted everyone to watch.

He allowed the kids to lick fingers-full from the edges of the ice cream machine after he had made a batch. He made thousands of gallons, packing

it in tall metal tubs. Until refrigeration, it was kept cold on blocks of ice.

"We still have one of those big, heavy tubs where I packed the ice cream, hauling it to picnics, parties or weddings," he says. "They were upright, so big that you could take a bath in them. They kept ice cream cold. We always had to work hard to make a living, but ice cream was a magic seller for us."

That magic brought in youngsters like Fred Larson of Moline. "I used to bike down to the Moline location when I was a kid on hot summer days with the change jingling in my pocket. I used to order a Bachelor's Kiss even before I knew what a bachelor was."

Lago's ice cream is irresistible. It is 12 percent butterfat. It is all homemade. If you order peach ice cream, someone has peeled fresh peaches for it. If it's strawberry ice cream, someone has plucked the little green stems from the berries.

Customers like Penny Weedon of Moline appreciate the hometown flavor. "I provide foster care for teens," she says. "I bring a youth to Lago's for our special alone time, and it has always been their first time here. Some of the toughest kids aren't so tough at Lago's — the little kid shows itself to me here."

'Whisker Puss' — a swimming pool of cream

Tom Sr. always named his cars. A 1951 Buick was called "Whisker Puss." It was regularly used to haul big milk cans of cream — not milk, but pure cream — from the dairy to the Moline store for making ice cream.

During his junior and senior years at Moline High School, Frank Ege worked at the store. He tells of one day when Tom had just returned from the dairy with 10-gallon cans of cream in the old Buick.

"Mr. Lagomarcino hopped out of the car behind the store and opened a rear car door. Two big milk cans of cream had fallen over... 20 gallons. A wave of cream ran out of the car. I can't ever remember Mr. Lagomarcino swearing, but he came as close as he ever did that day.

"He hooked up a hose and washed the inside of Whisker Puss. He had to hose off his shoes, too. Then, he got back into the wet car and went back to the dairy for another load of cream. Making deliveries in the old Buick was never the same after that. There was always a rank smell of sour cream in the car. If you didn't roll the windows down, the smell was enough to bring tears to your eyes — and then, there were the flies ..."

Famous Fountain Follies
and other heavenly sundaes

You never really know a person until you've shared a sundae. Some are meant for lovers, like the Loving Spoonful and Bachelor's Kiss.

There are sundaes to impress someone or make little ones happy and smear chocolate all over their faces.

Many were — and still are — named for celebrities. Some are for special

events, like Christmas and St. Paddy's Day.

At Lagomarcino's, imaginations are coaxed to go wild with sundaes. One menu from the 1940s is called "Our Famous Fountain Follies," with a Whooper Dooper that had fruit salad, ice cream, sugar wafers and pecans. The Zombie Split was finished off with salted nuts. Quad-City Special still has a steamboat paddlewheel made of cookies.

Through the decades, Lago's has played sundaes off names and fads, like the Black Bottom, a gooey sundae named after a dance, and the Etta Kett. Etta was a Diane Keaton-type who was in the comics pages from 1925 to 1974.

Spare change once went a long way in paying for a sundae, like on Halloween 1928 when a Strawberry Dream or Happy Thought was 20 cents — without nuts, 15 cents. Malted milks (hot or cold) were 15 cents, and it was a nickel more if the customer wanted a fresh egg cracked into them.

Tom Sr. always said, "To get a sundae here is an experience."

Calories will not count to read a brief chronology of Lagomarcino sundaes ...

Cool creamy tributes

Mt. Vesuvius

The most spectacular sundae ever made by Lago's was the Mt. Vesuvius. It was created by Uncle Charlie in the early 1920s, named after the volcano in Italy. It came in a tall soda glass with several scoops of ice cream, covered in a potpourri of toppings and enhanced with sliced bananas and whipped cream. Instead of a cherry, a sugar cube dipped in brandied alcohol was perched on the top. The server would light the sugar cube and the sundae took on the look of an erupting volcano. The flaming concoction would be hurried to the booth or table, while everyone in the place ooh-h-h-ed and ah-h-h-ed.

The Clara Bow

This sundae was named for the wild, sexy flapper of the silent movies. Lago's was the place to go after seeing a film at one of the five Moline theaters, and the Clara Bow was a hit sundae for more than a decade. One portion of fruit ice cream, a sliced ripe banana, one portion of vanilla ice cream, topped with whipped cream, pecan halves and a red maraschino cherry. Served with a pitcher of hot caramel sauce.

"I did it my way"

A sundae created especially for Frank Sinatra's farewell tour, a packed appearance at The Mark, now the i wireless Center. Doing it his own way, each customer took a hand at being a soda jerk. They could design their own sundae, choosing flavors of ice cream, toppings, nuts and bananas. A one-of-a-kind sundae.

Coco Banana

Created for Barry Manilow concerts in the Quad-Cities, this treat was named after his hit, "Copacabana." Sliced ripe bananas, two scoops of Dutch chocolate ice cream smothered in chocolate sauce, topped with shredded coconut, whipped cream and a red cherry.

Rocky Mountain High

A tribute to singer-songwriter John Denver. A double-dip of homemade rocky road ice cream, hot fudge sauce, whipped cream and the inevitable cherry.

Sweet Caroline

For The Mark's first concert on May 28, 1993, Lago's in Moline stayed open late. Customers were lined outside on the sidewalk to get a "Sweet Caroline Sundae" in honor of Neil Diamond, the opening night star. "You have to play to the crowd," said Tom Sr. A scoop of vanilla ice cream, a scoop of fresh strawberry ice cream, sliced banana, rich caramel topping and finished off with roasted pecans, whipped topping and of course, the maraschino cherry.

Big Top Sundae

This one is always a hit when Ringling Bros. and Barnum & Bailey Circus is playing the i wireless Center. A generous portion of vanilla ice cream, surrounded by animal crackers, choice of topping and a circus flag atop the whipped cream. Circus performers are big customers at the Moline store.

... and for the holidays

Frosty the Snowman

A big scoop of vanilla ice cream sporting a marshmallow cookie hat, a reindeer candy corn nose and a mini-chocolate chip smile.

Kris Kringle

Two dips of homemade mint chocolate chip ice cream, topped with whipped cream and always, that red cherry. Served with a pitcher of hot fudge sauce and a miniature candy cane dipped in dark chocolate.

Snowball

A scoop of Dutch chocolate ice cream covered with creamy marshmallow topping, whipped cream and Christmas sprinkles.

Loving Spoonful

For Valentine's Day, two scoops of rich, peppermint stick ice cream, topped with whipped cream and a chocolate heart, accompanied by a pitcher of hot fudge.

Luck of the Irish

A St. Paddy's combination that includes two scoops of mint chocolate chip ice cream, smothered with whipped cream, a green maraschino cherry and a gold coin, accompanied by a pitcher of hot fudge.

When Irish eyes are smiling ...

An Irish cream sundae is served with hot fudge sauce and a gold coin for luck.

All that jazz

Even Davenport's native son, Bix Beiderbecke, would smack his chops at this fountain treat. Two round notes of rich vanilla ice cream, covered to the tune of marshmallow and frosty fudge toppings, ending on a high note of roasted cashews, whipped cream and a bright red cherry.

'Yes, we have no bananas'

Above, the title of a hit tune of 80 or so years — a smash on the vaudeville circuit. Lagomarcino's is a luscious spot for sundaes. Bananas were as important as ice cream in the first days of Lago's — and still today.

One popular sundae is a Banana Split. Another is called a Happy Thought. Big difference: The banana is split longways for a Banana Split. For a Happy Thought, the banana is sliced in rounds.

When he first worked at Lago's, Bryan Dodds of Davenport was sent on a special assignment by Tom Jr. to get seven hands (clustered bunches of 10 to 12) bananas at the grocery store.

"Trying to make a good impression, I pretended to know what 'hands' meant," he laughs. "I came back with seven separate bananas. There is a big difference, I came to find out."

The difference in real lemonade

On any summer day, there may be six cases of lemons stacked in the fridges of the Lagomarcino soda fountains.

It is the real thing. Lemonade is made one glass at a time.

First, the individual lemon gets a few seconds in a microwave. The warmth coaxes more juice from the lemon. It is sliced, each side hand-squeezed in an old-fashioned pull-down squeezer. Simple syrup, a slurry of sugar and water, is added to the tall glass. Then, a dose of water and crushed ice. Only crushed ice, so as not to bruise the juice.

The burst of real lemon is surprising. There is no mistaking the real thing.

HERE IT IS FOLKS!

A BRAND NEW DRINK ... TO HELP QUENCH YOUR SUMMER THIRST.

In a Few Weeks, Young and Old, Rich or Poor, They'll All Be Drinking ...

LAGO

After tasting Lago you will agree that it is one of the finest and purest drinks on the market today.

●

ASK FOR A LAGO at your favorite fountain!

●

CREATED, MANUFACTURED AND ON SALE AT

Also On Sale at the Following Dealers:

MOLINE.
Anderson Drug Store, 1221 5th Ave.
Blackwell Cigar Store, 509 15th St.
Bonte Confectionery, 1401 15th St.
Hickey Bros. No. 7, 1531 5th Ave.
Hickey Bros. No. 9, 400 15th St.
Jericho's Drug Store, 401 15th St.
Schlegel's Drug Store, 508 15th St.
Simpson's Recreational Parlor, 1402 6th Ave.
Walgreen Drug Store, 425 15th St.
Weigandt's Confectionery, 1627 7th St.

DAVENPORT.
Hickey Brothers No. 1, 132 East 3rd.
Hickey Brothers No. 4, 108 West 3rd.
Hickey Brothers No. 8, 201 Brady
Schlegel's Drug Store, 220 West 2nd.
Schlegel's Drug Store, 105 West 3rd.

ROCK ISLAND.
Hickey Brothers No. 12, 1830 3rd Ave.
Schlegel's Drug Store, 1700 2nd Ave.
Schneider's Drug Store, 1801 38th St.

EAST MOLINE.
Chocolate Shop, 510 15th Ave.

GENESEO.
Geneseo Candy Kitchen

LAGOMARCINO CONFECTIONERY

1422 5th Ave., Moline

Dealers, for Lago—Call Lagomarcino-Grupe Co., Phone Kenwood 5170

Charlie Lagomarcino, the mixologist who intended to take on Coca-Cola and Pepsi.

Lago
A miracle soda pop that lost its fizz

Late at night, under a single bare light bulb in the basement of the Moline store, Charles Lagomarcino intently stirred his formulas for a "dream soda pop."

Uncle Charlie, they called him around the Moline place. He was the dreamer who convinced himself that the family was destined for bigger and better things than peanut brittle and fruit baskets.

Coca-Cola was making millions; Pepsi was an up-and-coming drink in a tall-necked bottle; everyone was loving that deep purple Grapette in a crinkly bottle.

In the 1920s, Charlie began mixing ingredients. Secretly, he would hide what he was stirring. Over the long years, Charlie concocted 25 separate

and distinct soft drink formulas. He narrowed it down to four quenching recipes and beamed to the family, "I think I have it." But a soft drink bottler in Rock Island turned down his four formulas.

Charlie was ready to give up. Still, he did not want to dump down the drain the quantity of liquids he had used in his four separate combinations. So he mixed them all together. All in one big crock, they produced the exact taste he wanted. He called it his "four-in-one" soda pop.

Now, Charlie had to figure out what proportions he had used in slurrying them all together. It took two days to solve the riddle.

But what's a drink without a name? One suggestion was Charlie's Special. Others were Teaser, Golden Root and finally, Lago. There would be advertising, and Charlie was dreamily thinking of billboards and trucks announcing — in big letters — "Here comes another load of Lago."

Charlie's big day came in 1934 when the Moline Dispatch printed: "Perfection of Lago, the new thirst-quenching soft drink which Charles Lagomarcino of Moline has originated and is manufacturing this summer, came about accidentally at a time when the young Moline candy maker was about ready to give up in despair."

The Rock Island bottling company began bottling Lago. Those who still remember say it tasted a lot like today's Dr. Pepper. It sold reasonably well in local soda fountains and grocery stores, and went over big at the Moline Lagomarcino's.

To his sorrow, Charlie found it was tough to buck the big boys. Sales could not even touch lesser-known brands like Chero-Cola and Whistle, and the national biggies, Coca-Cola, Pepsi and Royal Crown.

Production of Lago was stopped.

"I would give anything to find a bottle of Lago with its original label," says Tom Jr. "For the finder, I'll give all the cherry Cokes they want for life."

Aunt Mary, who kept things hopping

It's a big order of chocolates to describe Mary Lagomarcino. She had wavy hair and was short with dark, darting eyes that saw everything going on in the Moline soda fountain. A family member says, "I can see her now; she was round, with a shy smile."

She never married; her love was family and the Moline store. To generations of customers, she was simply "Mary" or "Aunt Mary." Never was she far away from the store, because she lived upstairs.

Mary was candy maker, sandwich maker, doer of all things. Her brother, Tom Sr., was the businessman. Her other brother, Charlie, was the creative one who dreamed up the gooey sundaes and named them after celebrities, holidays or even landmarks.

Mary grew up caring not just for customers, but especially family. When her mom, Luigia, died, it was her duty to care for her brothers. She would wring her hands in despair that she never had time for an education — she had to quit school after eighth grade.

As Tom Sr. grew up and took over the store, it was Mary who tended all things that required her touch. That was most everything. She personally packed all the chocolates, eyeing them closely.

Mary Lagomarcino at the soda fountain.

"She was very particular," says niece Beth Lagomarcino. "If a chocolate was not dipped correctly, the dipper heard about it."

Says Tom Sr. of his sister, "Gosh, she was a worker. She was non-stop at doing everything."

In 1929, a bunch of kids who called themselves the Depression Group would hang out at the store and pool their savings for a single dime glass of Coca-Cola. Helen Egan of Moline, who is 93, remembers how her brother, Bill, belonged to that group.

"Sometimes we would drop into the store," Helen recalls. "Mary worried, wanting to walk us home. We told her we were all right, but she insisted on walking us."

Students from Paul Norton School in Bettendorf traditionally make the trip to Lagomarcino's for Green Rivers when they study the 1920s, 1930s & 1940s. Among the students dressed up in period costumes: Haley Bannon, Mikey Trahan, Megan Sharkey and Jack Wells.

Green River
It's all in the wrist

It's as green as an Irishman's dream, sparkling and emerald. When it's sweaty Midwest hot, nothing goes down better than a Green River. The words "Green River" are as cool as a summer's front lawn.

No one doubts that Green River was introduced to the razz-ma-tazz Tri-Cities at Lagomarcino's Moline store about 80 or 85 years ago.

Tom Jr. stands these days at the marble-topped fountain, squirting into a tall glass some lemon-lime syrup flavoring that is the color of a green neon sign. To the very top of the glass, he fizzes in carbonated water. He is briskly stirring all the time.

"It's all in the stir; it's the wrist action that makes us better than the new

Green Rivers coming out in bottles," he says. "It doesn't take a rocket scientist to make a Green River, but the quick stir is the secret."

"When we serve a Green River to older customers, it's like a walk down memory lane," he says. "When we serve it to their grandchildren, they go wild. Kids love it."

It originally was a Chicago drink named after the Chicago River, which is dyed green every St. Patrick's Day. The drink was steeped in innocence for the soda fountain trade until bone-dry Prohibition came along, with speakeasies eager for a mix that would attract jazz flappers shimmying to the jazz of horn players like Davenport's Bix Beiderbecke.

Eddie Cantor, in the Ziegfeld Follies of 1921, penned a jingle to the soft drink. Old vaudeville programs show a photo of Cantor and a singing duo — Van and Schneck — crooning:

**"For a drink that's fine with a kick,
Try Green River. It's the only drink you should pick."**

When the thirsty nation became "wet" again in 1933, the manufacturers

had an instant hangover. They feared that the happy days of the Green River were over. They weren't. It held on stronger than ever as a soda fountain drink. Lago's offered Green River Floats. The post-Prohibition "spike" was a dollop of vanilla ice cream.

Atop the soda fountain at Lago's Village of East Davenport store is a fat Green River dispenser-jar.

At authentic soda fountains like Lago's in Davenport and Moline, the Green River is the second-most popular fountain drink, next to cherry Coke. Whether or not the soft drink can take credit is questionable, but there's a city called Green River in Wyoming; a Green River Community College in the state of Washington; and a Seattle-based rock band called Green River.

95

Romancing the rye bread

You can travel a thousand miles in America without finding a good slice of bread. At Lagomarcino's, the rye is as softly light and delicate as a maiden's hand, but not fragile. The crust is as crisp as a chip.

It is home-baked Swedish rye, which sounds a little incongruous being served in an Italian soda fountain. It is picked up daily from the woman who bakes it. It comes in long Pullman loaves and is sliced on a 60-year-old slicer, which might add some wistful flavor. An old typewritten Lago's menu shows that a Longhorn cheese or a peanut butter sandwich on rye cost only a dime.

Lago's rye is so delicious it can be a fooler. Elizabeth Langdon of East Moline, Illinois, remembers, "Richard, my grandson, would only eat white bread until we brought him to Lagomarcino's for lunch and he had a sandwich on their homemade rye bread. We did not tell him for a long time that it was not white bread."

Lago's rye came to be about 70 years ago when Mrs. John Dustin brought her best rye bread to the "ladies exchange" in Moline's New York Store, hoping to make some pin money. The Lagomarcino family bought it for their sandwiches.

"It's an old Swedish recipe, and I'll tell no one," she would tell friends. The ingredients were all in her head, not even in a cookbook. But age takes its toll on old Swedish cooks, and she revealed the process to the late Helen Butcher, who baked it from the original recipe for Lago's for 31 years. The secret recipe was passed to another baker, who makes it exclusively for the soda fountains at the two stores.

There are about as many stories about the rye bread as there are about the Lago's hot fudge sauce. Remembers Jill Feuerbach DiOrio, now of Winchester, Massachusetts:

"I was in sixth grade and just got braces. I had an egg salad sandwich on rye. The rye was so soft it didn't even hurt my teeth."

From left to right: Frank Nelson, Carl Kautz, Bud Kurtz, Jim Allemeier (seated), Joe Murphy, Bill Quaintance, Ken Roberts, and Joe Hanson.

Another cup, please
The 100-year-old Coffee Club

They begin traipsing in about 9 in the morning and the call to order comes immediately. There are coffee clubs that hang on at about every restaurant worthy of the name.

Lagomarcino's in Moline believes it hosts the oldest coffee club in the Quad-Cities. For many years, Mary Lagomarcino, the sister of Tom Sr. and a mainstay of the place all her life, was the official java pourer.

"From what we learn, there has been a Lago Coffee Club since the place opened, and that's a hundred years," says Beth Lagomarcino.

Once, it was about two dozen guys, businessmen, priests, hangers-on. No women were allowed.

"But Dot Buresh, that ageless Moline Dispatch columnist and reporter, wormed her way into the group. The only woman," Beth says.

She was the rose in the middle of the thorns. Until her death in 2007, she ruled the group. She called herself the duchess.

In its halcyon days, the Lago Coffee Club had two dozen members. Now, only six or eight are left. Times change. To those who still gather, age is not important. "Old age" is always 15 years older than they really are.

Winning the 'Oscar' of the food world

'... Moline's spiritual heart'

"There are two homegrown names that resonate above all others among the residents of Moline, Illinois. One is John Deere, the farm machinery manufacturer that has been the economic engine of this Mississippi River town since 1848. The other is Lagomarcino's, the Main Street soda fountain that has served as Moline's spiritual heart for nearly a century."

Above was an accolade on the nomination that won Lagomarcino's one of the most coveted food awards in all the land.

The proud people of Lagomarcino's knew they were good, but they popped their sugar-covered

Members of the Lagomarcino family when they received the coveted James Beard Foundation Award in New York City. From left, Carol Lagomarcino Babcock, Sandy Lagomarcino, Tom Jr., Beth Lagomarcino, Terry Otten and Lisa Lagomarcino Ambrose.

buttons when they were selected to receive the James Beard Foundation Award. It is likely the highest honor for food and beverage professionals.

Time magazine calls the James Beard Foundation Award "the Oscars of the food industry." The honor is named for the chef and food writer considered to be the father of American gastronomy.

Since 1998, there have been only 59 America's Classics Beard Awards. Only seven Midwest restaurants have received it. Lagomarcino's is one of them.

The nomination was made by Rick Nelson, food writer for the Minneapolis Star Tribune. He wrote of Lagomarcino's:

"The candy kitchen turns out all manner of treats, including a spectacular hot fudge sauce; the recipe, guarded as closely as any state secret, is such a locally revered commodity that it merits historic landmark status."

What others say about Lago's

"My favorite is Lagomarcino's … a Quad-City classic that gets my vote for America's most beautiful ice cream venue. It's a nostalgia-lover's dream, with gorgeous tile floors, mahogany booths, Tiffany-style lamps and a pressed-tin ceiling. And the treats can't be beat."

— *Money magazine,*
by Paul Lucas

"Lagomarcino's … is no reproduction soda shop, suffering from the cutes. This is a bona fide turn-of-the-century sweet shop, still run by descendants of the founders, that turns out high-quality chocolates and one of the best hot fudge sauces made."

— *Food Finds magazine*

"… The best old-fashioned ice cream parlor in the world is Lagomarcino's Confectionary in Moline, Illinois, where they have been serving banana splits since 1908."

— *National Geographic Traveler magazine*

"Receiving a Lagmarcino-filled Easter egg … is like getting a box of chocolate and being able to eat the box."

— *Saveur magazine*

"Started as a Moline, Illinois, candy store in 1908, Lagomarcino's is still renowned for hand-dipped chocolates, as well as fancy fruit baskets. You won't find better sponge candy anywhere."
— *Road Food*

"… The one thing you must try if you are a newcomer to Lagomarcino's is the hot fudge topping. Made from a recipe acquired in 1918 … this bittersweet, not-too-thick elixir is simply the best hot fudge in this solar system or any other."
— *Gourmet magazine*

"Lagomarcino's caters to chocolate lovers. In fact, gooey-rich chocolate ice cream concoctions have starred at the fountain since Angelo Lagomarcino bought a hot-fudge recipe from a traveling salesman for $25 … Tom and family still stir up the same recipe, and customers swear it's the best tasting hot fudge ever."
— *Midwest Living magazine*

"The thick, rich dark brown fudge is served piping hot in individual 2-ounce glass pitchers. That way, each customer can pour it at leisure — all at once or a little at a time — on two portions of homemade vanilla ice cream topped with whipped cream and a maraschino cherry."
— *United Press International*

Chocolate wisdom

A dish of Tom Sr.'s recollections, shared over a double dip of chocolate ice cream:

• "Our original Moline store … think of it, for a hundred years, that wonderful smell of chocolate and fruit. I wonder how many thousands of times I've asked myself, 'What would the world be without chocolate?' "

• "Always make a sundae that looks good. I tell the soda jerks that if it looks good, you know it will taste better."

• "It was a terrible job to deliver fruit baskets in the middle of winter. You needed a phone book, a flashlight and a Bible. If I slipped in the snow, I can still hear apples bouncing down a hill."

• Talking about his age: "I am a 1915 model and all my parts are out of warranty."

• When customers would ask how the store is doing: "We are doing thirteen knots with a bent prop."

• "The bank next door was First National Bank a long time ago, and now is Chase. They always wanted to buy our building for a parking lot. My dad, Angelo, was one of the original directors of First National. My sister, Mary, always gave them the cold shoulder. She said that Lago's was there before the bank."

• "When my mom, Luigia, died, I was just a little kid and went to Italy with my dad, Angelo. He went to Italy to find a new wife, Carmella. Italian kids didn't quite accept me while I stayed there, but I had one good friend, a dog. I named him Bread. Have you ever heard anything so crazy as a dog named Bread?"

• "When my mother died, she lay in state above the store, candles and flowers all around her. They used to do that in those days. My dad always said, 'When my time comes, don't take me home above the store. Don't take me up those stairs.' "

• "Things could get awfully busy, but I never got rattled. I always told the help, 'No one can enjoy the luxury of a temper.' The store is really a stage and a schoolroom for the kids who work here. You learn fast or get walked over. For a long time, the waitresses were not allowed to write down orders. They had to do it by memory. Finally, I agreed they could write it down, but they had to do it with class."

• "We always had cats around the store for a useful purpose. One liked to curl up on a warm steam pipe in the basement. He'd swat when anyone went by. He swatted Jack Horton once too many times. Jack tossed it in the freezer for half an hour. It didn't hurt the cat, but Jack got a good scratch out of it."

• "Everyone likes to be noticed. That's why I like to greet everyone in the store as a friend. Treat everyone special. All businesses would be better if they treated everyone special."

• "Our chocolates have no calories ... just energy units."

Thanks for the memories …

For their 100th anniversary, the two Lagomarcino stores put little cards on the counters and in the booths. "Help us with celebrating our centennial," the cards said. "We are looking for your memories and stories of coming to Lagomarcino's." As of the publication of this book, more than 800 memories have been submitted. Here is a taste of them …

The Mallo Cup baby

"When we were expecting our second child in 1983, I had a craving for Mallo Cups. Mallo Cups were not available in any stores. My husband, Ed, went to Lagomarcino's and they were able to have them special ordered. When our daughter, Audrey, arrived, my husband handed out Mallo Cups instead of cigars. One Sunday we went to St. Mary's Catholic Church and overheard someone saying: 'Look, there's the Mallo Cup baby.' "
— *Kendra Kennedy, Moline, Illinois*

'Those turtles were mine!'

"My favorite memory goes back 24 years when I received a five-pound box of Lagomarcino turtles following a hysterectomy. Several women in rooms near mine began parading into my room, even though they had just gone through stapling of their stomachs to lose weight. Each thought they needed one of my turtles. I got dressed, put on my makeup and told my doctor I was ready to go home. I didn't want to share those turtles. Those turtles were mine!"
— *Beverly Edwards, Silvis, Illinois*

Beverly Edwards

Chocolates from Lagomarcino's show up everywhere, even 20,000 feet in the air. John Blackburn of Moline shares a box of Lago chocolates with crew members on a mission in Iraq. His mother, Greta, shipped the candy to him.

Teacher and the smokers

"Going back 69 years, young girls who had taken up smoking puffed away until they saw their gym teacher enter Lago's. She was onto their game of sliding their lit cigarettes in their hands under the table. She, of course, would sit down with them and get into a lengthy conversation, waiting for them to either burn their fingers or drop the cigarettes."

— *Beverly Olson Rott, Chicago, Illinois*

'For my last meal ... '

"If I were ever in prison, and was asked what I wanted for my last meal, I'd say, 'Lago's egg salad sandwich.' When we moved to Moline in 1950, we had never heard of Lagomarcino's, but it didn't take long for us to find this wonderful place to take our children."

— *Genevieve Rafferty, Rock Island, Illinois*

A memory for a new generation

"I like sitting at the counter and drinking milk shakes and eating pickles and thinking that they are mouth guards."

— *Eric Stadelman, 10, Davenport, Iowa*

German fan returns the favor

"Recently, I was hosting good friends from Hamburg, Germany. There were only a few places I insisted that we visit, and Lagomarcino's was one of them. He is a medical doctor who also practices chiropractic in Hamburg. He loved his visit so much that when my husband and I were married, he arranged to have a basket of Lago goodies sent to our hotel."

— *Dr. Julie Johnson Latham, Moline, Illinois*

Yum-yum

"Yore canyd is dlishis and Iscream"

— *Melanie Kleine*
Bettendorf, Iowa

Tradition in Dad's memory

"Every Valentine's Day my Dad, Tom Stimpson, would stop in at Lago's to purchase candy for his daughters and granddaughters. It was always a great treat to receive a box of Lago candies — no matter where his 'girls' were living during those years.

He died in 2001, but I keep up his tradition. Every year I send a box of Lago candy to his 'Canadian Valentines' — his granddaughters who live in Canada. I do this in his memory and with his love!"

— *Terry Stimpson, Rock Island, Illinois*

First meal for a Q-C newcomer

"This was the first place I ever ate in the Quad-Cities. I came here for a job interview at KWQC and after it was over, my Great Aunt Alice took me to Lago's for lunch. It was great. That was almost 19 years ago!"

— *Sharon De Rycke, Davenport, Iowa*

Etiquette exam

"I would bring boyfriends to see if they were gentlemen enough to pass the 'Lago Test' of behavior. The ones that weren't, I would dump and be glad I did, too."

— *Barb Woodin, Moline, Illinois*

Looking forward to the dentist

"After our regular trips to the dentist's office in downtown Moline, my mother would reward us four children for a good checkup with a trip to Lagomarcino's for hot fudge sundaes, thus making a visit to the dentist something to look forward to."

— *Joe Larson, Davenport, Iowa*

Easing the misery of therapy

"My daughter, Jayne, was diagnosed with a rare cancer and during the summer of 2004 we ate lunch at Lago's once a week because Jayne liked the food and was suffering from the effects of cancer therapy. The best day of all was when Tom invited Jayne to come back with other members of the family and see how candy is made. She was in remission at the time and it was a very special day that I will forever remember. Thank you for the memories; she went to heaven on November 12, 2005."

— *Nancy Andreesen, Bettendorf, Iowa*

A treasure to keep

"Once, as we sat at the counter, my grandson, Will, said that when he grew up, he was going to give all his money to Lagomarcino's. That might seem like a foolish, childish thing to say. But I think he had recognized what a valuable thing is preserved here."

— *Wendy Bowles, Peoria, Illinois*

Please, no vocals during the lunch hour

There it is, the sweet sound of "As Time Goes By" … "You must remember this, a kiss is still a kiss." Or Glenn Miller's "Serenade in Blue." Or the 1946 hit, "To Each His Own." It is music to sip a soda by.

Rock or rap in a Lago soda fountain? Heaven forbid! Tom Sr. firmly sets the rules.

"Music must be sweet and soft so customers can relax," he says. "They want to hang loose."

Only the golden oldies are acceptable …the swing era. Tom does a little sway to listen to Miller's big band sounds, in homage to his favorite big band leader, who was born in Clarinda, Iowa, about four hours away as the crow flies from the two Lago stores.

"Good music gets you in the mood," he says.

He wants Miller's "Moonlight Serenade" to be played at least three times a day. The Glenn Miller oldie, "Little Brown Jug," is a bit too lively for a slow-motion sundae, but it is tolerated by Tom.

No one ever complains, because Lago's is as much of yesterday as Artie Shaw's "Begin the Beguine," which Tom always says, " … is good accompaniment to a thick chocolate malt."

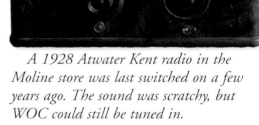

A 1928 Atwater Kent radio in the Moline store was last switched on a few years ago. The sound was scratchy, but WOC could still be tuned in.

There is one firm edict: During the lunch hour, between 11 a.m. and 1 p.m., no songs with vocals can be played.

"Customers want to talk to each other without being interrupted. They don't want to hear people singing," Tom Sr. says.

107

Chocolate nuggets

"Strength is the capacity to break a chocolate bar into four pieces with your bare hands — and then eat just one of the pieces."
— *Judith Viorst*

"Chocolate causes certain endocrine glands to secrete hormones that affect your feelings and behavior by making you happy. Therefore, it counteracts depression, in turn reducing the stress of depression. Your stress-free life helps you maintain a youthful disposition, both physically and mentally. So, eat lots of chocolate."
— *Elaine Sherman, "Book of Divine Indulgences"*

"I never met a chocolate I didn't like"
— *Deanna Troi in "Star Trek: The Next Generation"*

"It's not that chocolates are a substitute for love. Love is a substitute for chocolate. Chocolate is, let's face it, far more reliable than a man."
— *Miranda Ingram*

"All I really need is love, but a little chocolate now and then doesn't hurt."
— *Lucy, in the comic strip Peanuts, by Charles M. Schulz*

"I don't understand why so many so-called 'chocolate lovers' complain about the calories in chocolate, when all true chocoholics know that it is vegetable. It comes from the cocoa bean. Beans are veggies, 'nuff said."
— *Anonymous*

"I am a serious chocoholic. For the serious chocoholic, chocolate is better than sex. If you believe that, you really need to meet that special someone who can change your mind. If you have met that special someone and still believe that, I really need to know where you get your chocolate!"
— *Lora Brody, author of "Growing Up on the Chocolate Diet"*

"If not for chocolate, there would be no need for control top pantyhose. An entire garment industry would be devastated."
— *"The Rules of Chocolate," author unknown*

"Researchers have discovered that chocolate produced some of the same reactions in the brain as marijuana. The researchers also discovered other similarities between the two, but I can't remember what they are."
— *Matt Lauer on NBC's "Today" show*

"Simply put … everyone has a price. Mine is chocolate."
— *Dr. Ruth Westheimer*

Sweet Memories   Bill Wundram

Mary Mitchell of Port Byron, Illinois, dolled up in vintage finery for the century birthday of Lagomarcino's.

Kisses, ice cream and sweet memories

Block party celebrates 100th birthday of Angelo's dream come true

On a sunny summer afternoon, a block of Fifth Avenue in downtown Moline was blocked for a notable ice cream social. Well, maybe it wasn't exactly a social. More accurately, it was a love fest to celebrate the 100th birthday of Lagomarcino's first soda fountain.

111

Tony Hamilton's orchestra played all afternoon, but only big band songs from the 1940s.

It's no exaggeration to say 2,000 showed up to share the sweet memories. By count, 1,200 cups of ice cream were scooped from a soda fountain inside a white tent in front of the original store at 1422 Fifth Avenue. The temperature was a July-esqe 88 degrees, and the crowd went through 150 gallons of lemonade and 50 gallons of iced tea.

The street was jammed; the store was elbow-to-elbow with people who wanted inside the old place that really hasn't changed much in a century.

Old cars, like a 1911 Mitchell, were shiny in the parking lot next door. Women in flouncy old-time outfits and men in snappy summer straw hats listened to Tony Hamilton and his big band. Sixteen musicians, who sounded like the Glenn Miller band, offered only standards of the

Regular Lago customers like Dr. James Srail and his wife, Bernice, of Moline, celebrate the big day with sundaes.

The band played on.

1940s— tunes like "Tuxedo Junction" and "Serenade in Blue." There was actual dancing in the street.

Onto a platform stepped Tom Jr. He beamed, then called out:

"Now the party can officially begin. Mom and Dad are here."

He pointed to a smiling, waving Tom Sr. and Betsy Lagomarcino.

Tom Sr. is not as old as that first Lago store. He is only 92. The band played "Happy Birthday." Everyone sang, "Happy birthday to the store."

Tom Jr. laughed and pointed to the store: "If Grandpa Angelo ever was told his store would last 100 years, he'd have said that was nuts. He never intended it to last this long."

Betsy, Tom Sr. and Maureen Parsons, a Lago "alumni" employee, at the party.

It was a reunion for the 100th birthday of the Lagomarcino store. A Panama-hatted friend visits with (from left) Lisa Lagomarcino Ambrose, Abby Haggard, Columbus, Ohio, and Greta Dugan, Davenport. Abby came to Moline for the celebration.

It was a merry crowd on a perfectly perfect afternoon.

"It stormed last night," Tom Jr. said. "My mother prayed to every saint she knew — and some she didn't know — for good weather this afternoon. It was a blessing."

Tom Sr. never quit smiling. He leaned over to kiss his wife when the band played their favorite song, "Begin the Beguine."

This elder statesman of the soda fountain was engulfed. Women kissed him. Men shook his hand.

Agnes Molinelli of Rock Island kissed him on both cheeks.

"Tommy, you were best man at my wedding to my husband, John, 63 years ago," she said, kissing him a third time.

Constantly, the line was a dozen long to congratulate Tom Sr. and the store's 100th birthday. He acted young, like a kid soda jerk, eventually adjourning to the air-conditioned store. A line followed him. For three hours, he and well-wishers shared memories.

That night at home, exhausted, he said, "I had a ball. That was a humdinger."

Cool concentration at the anniversary street fest. More than a thousand cups of ice cream were served.

Beep! Beep! Antique cars, including a 1911 Mitchell, were nostalgic attractions of white wall tires and running boards.

Helen Egan and Helen VanHooreweghe visit a good friend.

Tom Sr., with son Paul, right, shares memories with friends, the young and the old.

Tents, instead of cars, lined a block of Moline's Fifth Avenue.

Snap! Hold it! Just one more picture.

Beth, Tom Jr. and Lisa

'This is where we belong'

(They came back)

It's a warm feeling. Chocolate runs in their blood. Lagomarcino's is all about family.

Today a son and two daughters from the third generation of Lagomarcinos run the show in Moline and in Davenport.

"Let's hope that a fourth generation will carry on," says Beth Lagomarcino.

Three of the six children of Tom Sr. and Betsy Lagomarcino — Tom Jr., Beth and Lisa — returned to the business after college and careers in other fields.

It's a unanimous feeling, "This is where we belong."

Tom Jr. was a special education teacher and later received his doctorate from the University of Illinois. In 1990, he felt the pull, an urge to return to the family business.

"My roots were there," he says. "I prayed a lot. I had my doubts. Dad was growing older. I worried if the store — we were just in Moline then — would continue without him.

"I was a part of the place. I gave up teaching and never looked back."

It's likely unprecedented that the thick malted milk you dip into at the Davenport store is made by a soda jerk with his doctorate in education.

Dad told the three, "I'm glad you came back."

> *"There is something in our blood in a place like this; it is a strong sense of family."*

Beth, with a master's degree, taught for eight years and returned to run the Moline store. "I worried that if anything happened to Dad, the place would be done. I came back because Lagomarcino's is an emotional place to us. We all grew up working in the store, but Dad discouraged us from going into the business. He told us, over and over, 'It's too much work.' I guess we never believed him. The store is in me."

Lisa Lagomarcino Ambrose, with a bachelor's degree in therapeutic recreation, came back to carry on the family line. "There aren't many traditions left in the Quad-Cities," she says while building a Swedish rye ham sandwich at the Davenport store. "There is something in our blood in a place like this; it is a strong sense of family."

With three members of the third generation returning to the business, there was no way the Moline store could involve all of them.

"That's when we decided to open another soda fountain in the Village of East Davenport," Tom Jr. says.

Tom Jr., Beth and Lisa have 10 children between them. Some from the fourth generation are working in the stores. Their parents are hopeful they will grow up wearing long white aprons and mixing Green Rivers.

Tom Sr. and grandson Lee

And the
story continues ...

To our readers,

Thank you for allowing us to share our *Sweet Memories* with you. Perhaps we've left you hungry for the taste of Lagomarcino's chocolate. You're in luck! While Lagomarcino's is a place steeped in family tradition, our turn of the century confectionary is just a click of the mouse away.

Visit us online at www.lagomarcinos.com

Chocolates

Our online catalog provides a great selection of the chocolates you've seen featured throughout this book. Choose from assorted chocolates, truffles, toffee, or pecan dainties. Depending on the season, you will also find our famous chocolate Easter eggs, sponge candy and Valentine hearts.

If you find yourself in the Quad-Cities, please join us during the busy lunch hour. As you're sitting in one of the gorgeous, handcrafted mahogany booths, you'll start to feel the certain calmness, and satisfying wistfulness as you begin to notice pleasant memories drifting quietly past your table – *Sweet Memories* smelling faintly of chocolate.

Lagomarcino's business service also will be happy to assist you with corporate gifts at holiday time or any time of the year. Call Beth at Lagomarcino's in Moline at 309-764-1814 or Lisa in the Village of East Davenport at 563-324-6137.

Where can I purchase additional Sweet Memories books?

Sweet Memories is available at both Lagomarcino's stores, and through our online catalog.

If you would like to purchase large quantities, contact us at 563-324-6137.

Lagomarcino's	Lagomarcino's
1422 5th Avenue	2132 East 11th Street
Moline, IL 61265	Davenport, IA 52803
Phone: 309-764-1814	Phone: 563-324-6137
Fax: 309-736-5423	Fax: 563-323-0846

www.lagomarcinos.com

121